Ross Sea

frozen sea ice

Cape Royds

Mt. Cis

Mt. Erebus

Mt. Terror

ROSS ISLAND

(PistenBully)

McMurdo Sound

Discovery Hut

McMurdo Station

Scott Base

Ross Ice Shelf

McMurdo Ice Shelf

Ice Runway

Brown Peninsula

Black Island

White Island

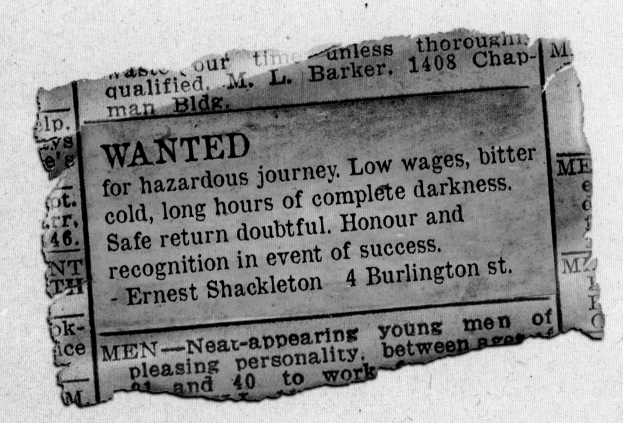

My ANTARCTICA

True Adventures in the Land of Mummified Seals, Space Robots, and So Much More

G. Neri

illustrated by Corban Wilkin

CANDLEWICK PRESS

When I was a kid, I dreamed of being an explorer.

I hoped to trek to the Poles or dive into the Mariana Trench or rocket to the Moon one day.

But it never happened.

11

Then I grew up and started writing books for kids—which unexpectedly landed me in the most extreme place on Earth: Antarctica. I was an explorer at last!

RCTICA

Okay, I know what you're thinking—how did I end up in the coldest place on Earth?

Well, it wasn't easy: (a) I live in Florida, (b) I was totally
unqualified, and (c) I don't even own winter clothes!

Most people who go to Antarctica are scientists and their support staff, but from the time I was a kid, I never did well in math and science. I found I had to simplify things in a way my brain could understand. Like, how do you tell the difference between the Arctic and the Antarctic? My answer: they're opposites—get it?

Bears!

Santa!

ARCTIC

{ water underneath }

Ice 3-12 feet thick

North

South

{ land underneath }

ANTARCTIC

ice 9,000 feet thick

Penguins!

No Santa.

Simplifying these ideas allowed me to translate science in a way that other kids could understand, too.

Somehow I managed to convince the National Science Foundation to send me to Antarctica so that I could write about the experience in a way that inspires my readers.

The first question I had was, *How do you even get to Antarctica?* Well, after a year of planning, I flew 21 hours from North America to New Zealand, then got in one of those giant military cargo planes you see in movies to fly 5 *more* hours to the Ice.

The first time I see Antarctica, it's out of a tiny porthole in the back of the plane.

It looks like a frozen planet.

I feel weird sitting on the plane surrounded by all these important scientists on their way to solve life's greatest mysteries. And it's mind-numbingly LOUD!

BBBRRRZZZZZZZZZZZZZZZZZZZZZZ

What am I even doing here? Antarctica is no Florida and I am no scientist.

Then something strange happens. We land right on the ice, and my doubts turn to awe as soon as we step off the plane.

It feels like setting foot on the Moon.

I feel ready to try to understand this strange and
beautiful place so that I can help unlock the mysteries
of the continent for you.

The first thing I notice is that all the science people here seem to be looking for answers to life's big questions.

Antarctica brings out the 10-year-old in me—
like I'm discovering everything for the first time.

I can't help but feel like that kid who dreamed of
being an explorer so long ago.

Everywhere I look, there's something
I've never seen before.

I spend a lot of my time in a place called McMurdo Station, the main hub for US science in Antarctica. Most of the 800–1,100 Americans coming to the Ice each year stay at least a week here.

The odd thing about McMurdo: it sits at the base of an active volcano called Mount Erebus! This seems like a bad idea until they tell me that it's open at the top like a giant bowl, allowing all that heat and pressure to vent. While it never erupts, it occasionally spits out a small lava bomb or two . . . but at the station, we're safe.

WELCOME TO
McMurdo
EST. 1956

Elaine, our guardian on the Ice!

The only other artist grantees here are Kirsten and Michelle, who I share a lab space with. They draw ocean species while diving under the sea ice!

SCOTT, MY ROOMIE

McMurdo Station reminds me of college: I sleep in a dorm (see * in photo) with my roommate, Scott, a precipitation scientist who's here to count snow! I train, work in the lab, worry about who to sit with in the cafeteria, go to the gym, relax in the lounge watching bad movies, and try to make new friends.

Here are places I might go to on any given day:

1. The food galley, the main hub of life here. The food is amazing—everything from Sunday brunch with brisket to Thai shrimp curry to burger and burrito nights. Because people work around the clock, you can order pizzas to-go 24 hours a day!

2. Also in the big blue building: a small gift store, a barbershop, a crafts room, a radio station, and the most remote ATM in the world

3. A small library, where you can read Antarctic classics like *The Worst Journey in the World*

4. Skua Hut (free thrift store for anything from old boots and socks to used Santa costumes)

5. An old officers' club (now a coffee house) with a workout gym next door

6. An old indoor basketball court (with a rock climbing wall)

7. Crary Labs, where science teams bring their samples back to study

8. Dive Locker, where divers hang out and prep

9. Helo pad, where you can take off to go to remote locations

10. Training school

11. Snowmobiles be here.

12. Camping depot, where you can check out gear in a backpack almost as big as you

13. Fire station—always check in before heading into the wild

14. General Hospital

15. Yacht Club (with no yachts)

16. Chapel of the Snows (One of my friends got married there!)

17. Live video hookup area, where I talk to schools back in the US

18. Ob Hill (where there's a giant cross honoring Captain Scott and his men)

19. Shuttle stop, where you can head over to New Zealand's Scott Base or ice shelf locations

20. Road to Discovery Hut (the first explorers' hut)

Note: By the time you read this, the old station will have been torn down and replaced with a newer, more modern base.

This is how you dress in Antarctica. It's called
Extreme Cold Weather (ECW) gear. You even
have to wear it on the plane!

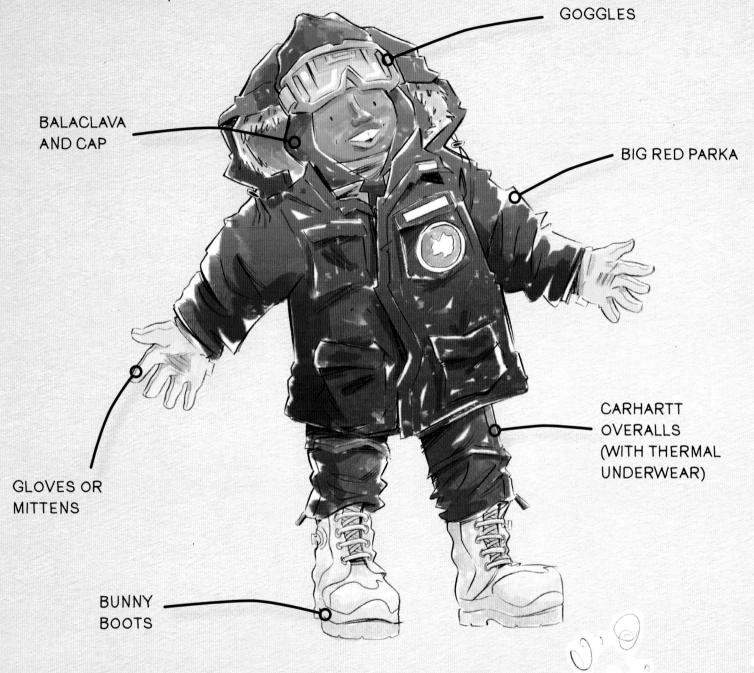

GOGGLES

BALACLAVA
AND CAP

BIG RED PARKA

CARHARTT
OVERALLS
(WITH THERMAL
UNDERWEAR)

GLOVES OR
MITTENS

BUNNY
BOOTS

They also give me a cool radio handle to boot. (*This is
Whisky-480. Over.*) Just like a real explorer.

Since this is the most extreme place on Earth, I have to do a whole week of special training before I start exploring. In Antarctica, safety first. Your life depends on it!

learning how to secure a tent

learning about emergency rescue procedures

practicing rappelling into a crevasse

helicopter safety training

studying cracks in the ice for safe passage

One of the first things I notice is that no one really looks like an explorer. Or at least the ones I think of from the olden days. People here look like regular people. Some are young, some old (one of the scientists is 81!). There's a mix of men and women, mostly white, but I see a few folks of color like me. There are a lot of science people, but many others have regular jobs, like chef, janitor, mechanic, firefighter, carpenter, doctor, plumber, and even barber!

Because it's so hard to get here, no one seems to complain much, even while they're hard at work.

I may be cleaning toilets and dishes, but I'm cleaning them in Antarctica!

Looks can be deceiving. One woman who seems like a cheerful librarian turns out to be the Indiana Jones of the Ice. She's a mechanical engineer for ice structures and is part of the South Pole traverse team. Her job: searching for hidden crevasses. She sometimes has to climb down into them to blow them up so her team can safely pass!

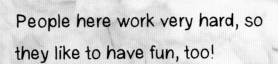

People here work very hard, so they like to have fun, too!

Antarctica is an entire continent devoted solely to science. It's like a frozen museum! Scientists are looking at five basic things: Earth, its history, its living creatures, how it all works together, and even outer space!

THE GEOPHYSICIST

"The ice shelf here is the biggest piece of ice in the world, and when that melts, it will drastically change the map of the Earth."

THE PALEOBOTANIST

"One of the big surprises for people is that, millions of years ago, Antarctica was free of ice, and different landscapes hosted all kinds of plants and animals, including dinosaurs."

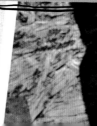

THE SEAL BIOLOGIST

"We're trying to understand how many animals are here, how that's changing over time, and why some live longer and produce more offspring than others."

THE GEOCHEMIST

"I use isotopes to reveal information about the ages and origins of rock, air, or water. They're like radioactive clocks in the rocks."

THE ASTROPHYSICIST

"Antarctica is an ideal place to explore space from. We're tracking cosmic rays to determine the origin of the universe."

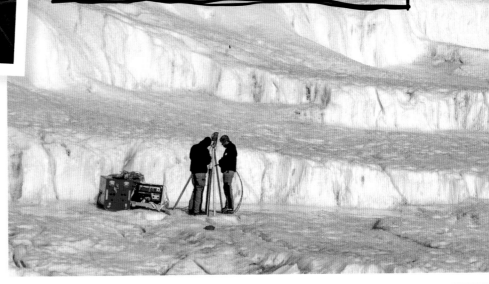

My job down here is to follow different science teams into the field to try to understand what they do.

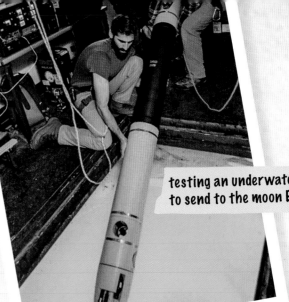

testing an underwater robot to send to the moon Europa

working on a long duration air balloon to capture cosmic rays

collecting ice sheet data by remote sensing radar

preparing to dive underneath the ice shelf

installing an undersea webcam to study life under the ice

collecting ocean specimens

listening to rocks crack to study erosion

using a robot to probe for crevasses on Mount Erebus

conducting laboratory experiments

sifting for foraminifera

studying layers of ice to look back in time

41

A lot of the details of scientists' work goes over my head. So when I talk to them, I like to start at the beginning.
Then it's just like we're two kids talking to each other.
When was the first time science or nature exploded in your brain?
I remember the first time I saw the moons of Jupiter through a telescope. Where I grew up, we had the most amazing skies. I knew my constellations because my dad was a paratrooper who knew how to navigate by night sky . . .

Slowly I begin to understand
why they do what they do.

When I was a kid, my dad's best friend was a carpenter down here, and once, he brought me a big book about Antarctica. That book grabbed me so much, I just really got into the idea of the South Pole and everything—and he'd tell us crazy stories, too. I guess it's why I became so interested in snow and ice . . .

THE BIG BOOK OF ANTARCTICA

The days are long and hard. Actually, a "day" is my whole visit—almost two months long, since the Sun never sets in Antarctica at this time of year.

Time feels both fast *and* slow. Sometimes days seem like weeks, and other times, hours are like minutes.

A couple of friends get frostbite (they heal). We all get sick with this thing called The Crud (that's what it feels like). And I miss my family.

When I call home, it feels like I'm in a different dimension. Because of the difference in time zones, it's eight hours later for my family (but a day earlier—blame the international date line). This is the longest I've ever been away.

Sometimes when I video call, my computer freezes—literally. I have to put my laptop inside my jacket so my body heat can warm it back up. In a weird way, it's like hugging them again.

When I wonder why I'm really here, I remember that writers and artists have been coming to the Ice since the beginning. Somebody needs to pick up where they left off and tell the story of this place, its science, and the amazing people here.

Why not me?

Herbert Ponting, expedition photographer and cinematographer for Captain Scott's Terra Nova Expedition

an account from Ernest Shackleton

Apsley Cherry-Garrard, part of Captain Scott's team and author of *The Worst Journey in the World*

Cape Crozier by Edward Wilson

Herbert Ponting in action

So, I say YES whenever someone asks me if I want to go someplace, meet somebody, or experience something special. It's how I find stories.

fake emergency drill

snowmobiling across the frozen sea

fishing for specimens

helicoptering

penguining

hiking across lava beds

trying not to get frostbite

collecting glacier berries to melt for water

climbing down under the sea ice

Being here gets my imagination going . . .

It makes me want to walk in the footsteps of the great explorers, discovering new wonders never seen before.

Like joining the traverse team to trek 28 days to the South Pole.

Or capturing cosmic rays with a long duration balloon to find the origin of the universe.

It makes me want to dive
under the ice into the clearest
water on Earth

(where extreme cold and
high oxygen levels cause
polar gigantism, which means
everything is bigger).

Or ride a Zodiac boat across the frozen sea.

Or see those strange nacreous clouds form when the Sun rises after many months of total darkness.

For sure, I want to know
why Blood Falls is red.

Or why when you cut into a meteorite
found near Nimrod Glacier, it looks
like stained-glass icebergs.

I want to know how these
amazing penguins are affected
by climate change . . .

and what we can do to slow down the melting of the ice.

I want to see and know it all,
to experience Antarctica in
all its beauty and wonder.

I find myself taking endless pictures of the icy horizon . . .

because every time I look at it, it's different.

I also make videos of my feet as they walk across the ice, the snow, the lava rocks, and the dirt—because I'm in awe of all the amazing textures and sounds they make as I trek across Antarctica.

(Sometimes I look at penguin tracks, too.)

I record sounds so I won't forget:
the soulful calls of seals wafting up
from under the sea ice.

The crackle of interference on a
satellite phone from meteorites
passing through the atmosphere.

The sound of pressure ice snapping
and popping.

Even the sound of true silence,
so quiet I can hear my heart beat
in my ears.

Sometimes I laugh out loud from the
sheer spectacle of it all.

All this information makes my head hurt. But I have a notebook called *My Brain* where I try to make sense of everything.

To figure out how this place works, I start making lists of things I come across. Here are a few:

THINGS YOU WON'T FIND IN ANTARCTICA:

- polar bears (see N. Pole)
- grass
- trees
- people on smartphones
- Starbucks
- dogs or cats
- fast food
- malls
- schools
- pets
- traffic jams
- guns
- rain!
- night (in summer)
- day (in winter)
- bugs
- kids
- blazing internet!

THINGS YOU WILL FIND:

- dorms
- a galley cafeteria
- a free thrift store (Skua Hut)
- a church
- two libraries
- a wine bar/coffee shop
- 3 gyms
- a basketball court w/climbing wall
- a giant science lab
- a radio station
- a gift store
- a barber
- handwashing stations
- aquarium
- helicopter pad
- arts-and-crafts room
- a yacht club
- offices w/cubicles
- an ATM

LIST 2: VEHICLES OF ANTARCTICA

Since it's so tricky to travel on all that snow and ice, people have to be inventive in how they move from point A to Z.

ATV carrying a whole science team

helicopter (or helo)

The Hagglund

a Zodiac nearing a marine research vessel

Ivan the Terra Bus

LIST 5: CRITTERS OF ANTARCTICA

Antarctica is home to more than just penguins, seals, and whales, with some of the most unique sea creatures in the world.

feathered sea star

sea angel

jellyfish

giant sea spider

scale worm

octopus

LIST 7: UNIFORMS OF ANTARCTICA

While most people wear Big Red, you'll see plenty of other outfits on the Ice.

Big Red

firefighter's uniform

cold water dry suit

military uniform

microbiologist haz-mat suit

baker's uniform

one-piece heavyweight snowsuit

penguin costume

LIST 11: SPORTS AND RECREATION

People in Antarctica work hard, which means they need to do something fun to unwind. Luckily, you can do everything from sports (softball, basketball, marathon racing, biking) to relaxation (yoga, tai chi, music) to friendly competitions against the New Zealand station next door (rugby, manhauling, tug o' war)!

LIST 18: TOILETS OF ANTARCTICA

Just like camping in any pristine area, there is a strict "pack it out" rule when it comes to, um, relieving yourself. Believe it or not, all human waste from Americans gets collected, processed into powder cakes, and shipped all the way back to the US of A!

rocket toilets (incinerate waste!)

tent toilet

room with a view

outhouse

pee bottle

tandem

LIST 31: ICEBERGS SHAPED LIKE THINGS

couch

sea monster

swans

cat

submarine and ship

big head

LIST 35: WEIRD THINGS I SAW IN ANTARCTICA

tomato plants growing from a box of dried human waste (the only plant life I ever saw)

metal chain sculpture of an orca

lots of big crosses for people who died

seal teeth shaped like flames

rock concert

infrared telescope to see invisible auroras

Fata Morgana (ice mirage)

LIST 39: THINGS YOU'LL FIND IN AN EXPLORER'S HUT

Since Antarctica is the coldest and driest place on Earth, things
don't rot or decay; everything is literally frozen in time. The explorers'
huts are just as they were left over 100 years ago!
It's the only place I've ever felt like I was time traveling!

an explorer's boot

me pretending to warm up next to an old stove

science instruments

cargo box

matchstick lighter

science experiment
abandoned upon rescue

LIST 43: THE STRANGE AND WONDERFUL STRUCTURES OF THE ICE

Cold weather means shelter and unique structures for science.

an airfield control tower

camp at Explorer's Cove

the "Apple" emergency shelter

NASA satellite dish, aka the "Golf Ball"

observation tube, aka "ob tube"

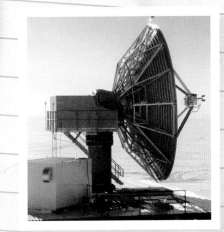

South Pole Marisat-GOES Antennae

Some experiences can't be captured on a list,
but there are a few that I'll never forget . . .

Like that time we were trapped in a
helicopter over the frozen sea, running
out of fuel and surrounded by Condition
One storms.

Or that time we trekked where no
human had ever walked before.

Or when I slept at the foot of a glacier listening to it calve at night.

Or when I woke up in the same kind of tent that the explorers Scott and Shackleton used and stared out at the same pluming volcano they saw over 100 years ago.

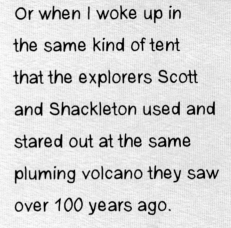

Or how I had so many penguin encounters, they started calling me the penguin whisperer.

Or that time I set out on a Holy Grail trek with my guide,
Jarod, and found the mythical pickax supposedly driven
into the top of a volcanic cone, like King Arthur's sword,
by Ernest Shackleton.*

*It turned out to be one of Captain
Scott's team members' axes
instead! Although I wished I could
hold it, I respected its place in
history and left it untouched.

Or that time I paid tribute to a long-ago friend who'd perished here many years ago. It was his yearning to dive underneath the ice in Antarctica that got me dreaming about coming here . . .

MARK · N?
MACMILLIAN
NEW HARBOR
ANTARCTICA
14 NOV '87

Thinking of Mark makes me think
about the most important thing of all
in Antarctica: the PEOPLE.

They say the world is like a snow globe, and when
you shake it, all the dreamers, outsiders, risk-takers,
and folks who don't belong anywhere else settle at the
bottom, in Antarctica. Like Mark. Like me. Like everyone
down here, it seems.

Maybe that's what helps people work so well together: everyone's in the same boat and needs everyone else to survive and get work done. The only boss here is Mother Nature, and you better listen to her!

In the end, Antarctica feels like a dream to me. I came down here hoping to write something that captured this strangely wonderful world of the Ice.

This is what I wrote on the flight home:

When I first arrived in Antarctica

I felt like a brown boy in the whitest place on Earth.

At first sight,

Antarctica is sooo white.

In a storm,

The ice is white

The sky is white

The people are white.

But when the weather clears

You see the bluest sky

You see a rainbow in the ice

And the people are the most colorful on Earth.

After seven weeks here,

I think I've finally discovered
    the real heart and soul of
    this place:

It may be the most extreme, faraway spot on the planet . . .

                    but it feels like home.

FINAL LIST FOR ANTARCTICA:

Things you leave behind . . .

AUTHOR'S NOTE

I didn't really have a head for science when I was a kid. I was, however, immensely curious and loved to hear stories about the old explorers, like Ernest Shackleton and Robert F. Scott, and people I grew up watching on TV, like Jane Goodall, Dian Fossey, Jacques Cousteau, and the astronauts. Even though they didn't look like me, I loved the idea of someone being called to a faraway place completely opposite from their world and learning all about it as they explored. It usually changed their lives. Maybe that's why I dared myself to apply for an Artists and Writers grant from the National Science Foundation to go to Antarctica. I wanted to be an explorer, too.

Back in 2017, I was writing books for and working with a lot of kids from urban areas, some of whom had never really experienced nature or, like me, didn't do well in science. So I decided I would immerse myself in the world of the Ice and become a science translator, telling stories in a way that would have inspired me as a kid.

I was so taken by my time down there that I teamed up with other past grantees to form the Antarctic Artists and Writers Collective (www.aawcollective.com) so you can see how others used their artistic talents to tell the story of Antarctica, too.

There are many ways to get to the Ice. If I can do it, you can, too. I hope some of you will be inspired to go there yourselves when you grow up.

FACTS AND STUFF

Antarctica is BIG.

It's bigger than the US and Mexico combined (5.5 million square miles/14 million square kilometers), but instead of having 460 million people, Antarctica has only 5,000 humans at its busiest season, spread over the entire continent! It's the emptiest place on Earth. It is also the coldest, driest, windiest, overall highest, and most extreme place on the planet (which maybe explains the empty part). Even though it's 98% covered in snow and ice, it's the largest desert in the world—a polar desert, with ice as thick as three miles (almost five kilometers) deep. Its highest point is the peak of Mount Vinson, at 16,050 feet (5,000 meters); its lowest point is 11,500 feet (3,500 meters) deep, under the Denman Glacier—the deepest land point in the world.

Antarctica was the last continent to be discovered (1820). It's the least walked-upon continent on Earth but also the most well-mapped. Antarctica has 24 time zones, all of which meet at the South Pole (though in practice, McMurdo is on the same time as Christchurch, New Zealand, since that's the last stop for everyone heading to the Ice). It also has 24 hours of either sunlight or darkness—depending on the time of year. People cannot stay on the Ice for much more than a year before returning to the mainland to allow their bodies to recover from the darkness and cold. The cold is so harsh that it actually changes your body chemistry, which can result in some short-term memory loss. There are no people who are from Antarctica, but many still call it home.

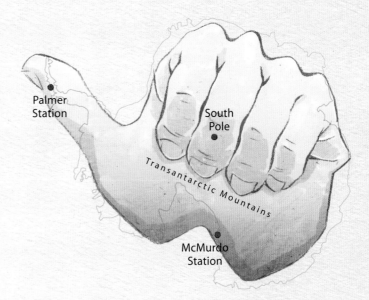

My handler, Elaine, likes to show us where things are in Antarctica by using her handy-dandy hand map!

An international treaty signed in 1959 made Antarctica the only continent dedicated to the peaceful pursuit of science without claims to territory (meaning no one can own the Ice). About 30 countries have research stations down there, pursuing such sciences as biology, glaciology, paleontology, Earth science, ecology, astrophysics, particle physics, space weather, oceanography, and atmospheric science.

The first artist to go in search of Antarctica was William Hodges, who joined Captain James Cook's second voyage to the end of the world in 1772. His painting of icebergs was the first known eyewitness depiction of the southern continent.

Likewise, Robert F. Scott and Ernest Shackleton both took artists and writers on their expeditions to tell the story of their exploits, which made headlines back in the early 1900s. To entertain themselves during the long, harsh winters, Scott's team created a magazine, the *South Polar Times*, and for the winter of 1908, Shackleton brought a printing press to the Ice to make a book, *Aurora Australis*. The Antarctic Artists and Writers Program continues this tradition, having brought over 125 creative people to the Ice over the last 40+ years. As of 2023, it will be called Polar STEAM. In 2019, the Antarctic Artists and Writers Collective was formed to exhibit and share these amazing artists' work with the public.

BIG QUESTIONS ABOUT ANTARCTICA!

WHO gets to go there?

The population is roughly 30% scientists and 70% support personnel—and maybe one or two people like me. Tourists can visit, but only for brief excursions along the coastline.

How do you EAT?

Food is shipped once a year, and they keep a three-year supply in a giant warehouse freezer. There are amazing cooks here, so you eat well!

Why doesn't the SUN set?

During its summer, Antarctica is on the side of Earth tilted toward the Sun, causing constant 24-hour sunlight. In the winter, Antarctica is tilted away from the Sun, causing 24 hours of darkness.

How do you SLEEP?

Poorly, in a tent or dorm room, often with a sleep mask covering your eyes to keep the sunlight out.

Is there WI-FI?

Um, not really. Your phones are useless here. There is internet at the stations, but it's so slow that you can't watch any streaming media, and if you want to email a single photograph, it might take a while. It's the equivalent of making your phone a hot-spot and sharing it with 1,000 people.

Are there HOTELS and RESTAURANTS?

No! At the stations, there's a main cafeteria, or galley, that feeds everybody, and if you go to a remote camp, you have to bring your own food.

Being away from family is the hard part, but what keeps me coming down here is all the science and engineering—one little tweak to some equation can actually save a life.

What is a MUMMY SEAL?

It's a mummified seal, hard as a rock—and even if it's hundreds or thousands of years old, it won't have decomposed too much because it's been freeze-dried by the coldest, driest place on Earth. A mummified seal might be the result of a young pup getting separated from the group in a storm and wandering off in the wrong direction, potentially ending up many miles from the water, where it perishes and freezes.

What DINOSAURS were discovered in Antarctica?

Over ten species have been discovered in the Transantarctic Mountains and on James Ross Island—most famously the Cryolophosaurus, aka Elvisaurus because of its crested pompadour. Dinosaurs still roam the Ice—in the form of penguins!

What are COSMIC RAYS, and why use balloons to capture them?

Cosmic rays are basically stardust from the Big Bang. They're clues to the origins of the universe. Scientists use long duration air balloons that ride the winds to circumnavigate the continent, staying up without intervention and delivering stardust particles back to the scientists like a boomerang.

How COLD does it get?

Hm . . . −40°F (−40°C) in summer, −76°F (−60°C) in winter. But it's a dry −76°F. The coldest recorded temperature in Antarctica was −128.6°F (−89°C).

How do you not FREEZE to death?

Wear your Extreme Cold Weather gear, follow safety rules, hydrate, and always have a field buddy with you outdoors.

Is Antarctica really a DESERT?

Yes! It's a polar desert and the largest desert in the world. In fact, it's so dry, people can go weeks without showering. They don't sweat and therefore tend not to smell, either.

Why is BLOOD FALLS red?

While not all the details are known, scientists believe Blood Falls emerges from a hill that's rich in iron, so the water oxidizes and turns red when it reaches the surface, much like rust.

How DANGEROUS is it, really?

The extremes of Antarctica can be very dangerous. That's why everyone does safety training every time they go to Antarctica. Everyone has to radio in before and after all outdoor treks to keep safe. Missed check-ins will turn into rescues!

Did that PICKAX really belong to Shackleton?

No, me and a friend, Jerod Knox, were able to determine it had been left by one of Captain Scott's Northern Party members in 1912, marking a food depot they'd rediscovered after having survived their winter in a snow cave.

How do you avoid getting hit by LAVA BOMBS?

Even though it would be your natural instinct to run away, scientists encourage you to face the volcano and pretend you are a center fielder tracking a fly ball. That way, you can get out of the lava bomb's way before it lands!

What is a Condition One STORM?

Antarctica has its own storm rating system. Condition One means extreme weather—seek shelter immediately!

What's a SEA ANGEL?

Sea angels are these tiny alien-looking beings that are a form of polar sea slug. They are see-through, gelatinous creatures with wings—very ethereal.

What's a GLACIER BERRY?

When glaciers calve off large chunks of ice, we call them glacier berries and collect them to melt for drinking water when in remote camps. Glacier water is the best! Carrying these large chunks of ice back to camp—the worst.

Antarctica changes your DNA. There are no distractions like phones and parking and finding times to meet up. Here, you eat, work, and play together. It's intense.

Out on location, we're the most remote people in the world. It's like the poor man's space program.

What causes AURORAS, NACREOUS CLOUDS, and FATA MORGANAS?

All are forms of atmospheric disturbances. Auroras (or aurora australis) are a natural light show in the atmosphere caused by storms on the Sun that disturb electrons in the Earth's magnetic field. In 24-hour sunlight, they are still there, but only visible using special ultraviolet (UV) instruments. Nacreous clouds (or mother-of-pearl clouds) form when the temperature in the upper atmosphere falls below −108°F (−78°C), which turns the moisture in the air into super-cooled liquid or ice crystals. Light is refracted by the ice crystals in the clouds, producing the shimmering iridescent rainbow effect found during the Winfly season, when the Sun first emerges after five months of darkness. Fata Morganas are ice mirages named for Arthurian sorceress Morgan le Fay. They occur when a layer of warmer air falls on colder dense air, acting like a refracting lens and inverting the image of whatever objects lie beyond it.

Why do you have to carry a PEE BOTTLE?

There is a strict "no yellow snow" policy. We need to keep everything as pristine as possible—even if it makes it harder for women in remote camps.

How dangerous is FROSTBITE?

Back in the explorer days, when access to medical care was more precarious, an appendage with frostbite would turn black and potentially fall off—toes, fingers, even noses. But these days, more is known about treatments. With immediate transport back to a doctor, frostbite can be relatively straightforward to treat.

Who DISCOVERED Antarctica?

It is believed that as far back as the seventh century, Maori explorer Hui Te Rangiora reached Antarctica, describing a dark and misty place with tall, bare mountains that "pierce the sky." Among Westerners, Captain James Cook was the first to venture past the Antarctic Circle in 1773, passing islands and icebergs, but failing to reach the continent. Russian explorers Fabian Gottlieb von Bellingshausen and Mikhail Lazarev were the first to see the continent of Antarctica in 1820. The first landing was probably a year later when American Captain John Davis set foot on the ice. The Heroic Age of Antarctic Explorers kicked off with the race to the South Pole, with many failed attempts by Captain Robert Falcon Scott and Ernest Shackleton's expeditions. Norwegian Roald Amundsen beat them both in 1911. When Scott finally reached the Pole a month later, he was shocked to find a Norwegian flag and tent. Scott famously wrote in his diary, "Great God! this is an awful place."

RECOMMENDED SOURCE MATERIAL

Books

Cherry-Garrard, Apsley. *The Worst Journey in the World*. Skyhorse, 2016.

Grill, William. *Shackleton's Journey*. Flying Eye Books, 2014.

Lester, Alison. *Sophie Scott Goes South*. Houghton Mifflin Harcourt, 2013.

Neri, G., and Corban Wilkin. *The Time Traveling Dino Detectives of Antarctica*. Ice Boy Comics, 2021.

Rogers, Susan Fox. *Antarctica: Life on the Ice*. Solas House, 2007.

Scott, Robert Falcon. *South Polar Times*. Folio Society, 2018.

Shackleton, Ernest H. *Aurora Australis*. Seto Publishing, 1988.

Walker, Gabrielle. *Antarctica: An Intimate Portrait of a Mysterious Continent*. Houghton Mifflin Harcourt, 2013.

Young, Karen Romano. *Antarctica: The Melting Continent*. What on Earth Books, 2022.

Films/TV

Clark, David, dir. *Dinosaurs of Antarctica*. Giant Screen Films, 2021.

Herzog, Werner, dir. *Encounters at the End of the World*. Discovery Films, 2008.

Ponting, Herbert, dir. *The Great White Silence*. Herbert Ponting, 1924.

Powell, Anthony, dir. *Antarctica: A Year on Ice*. Music Box Films, 2013.

Saks, Caitlin, and Arlo Pérez. *Antarctic Extremes*. NOVA and PBS Digital Studios, 2020. https://www.pbs.org/wgbh/nova/series/antarctic-extremes/.

Websites

Antarctic Artists and Writers Collective. "Antarctic Artists and Writers Collective: Exploring Antarctica through the Arts." www.aawcollective.com.

National Science Foundation polar grants for artists, writers, and educators. "Polar STEAM." https://polarsteam.info.

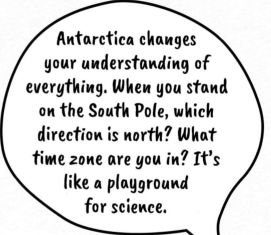

Antarctica changes your understanding of everything. When you stand on the South Pole, which direction is north? What time zone are you in? It's like a playground for science.

ACKNOWLEDGMENTS

Big thanks to the National Science Foundation Artists and Writers Program grant for making this possible! And thank you to all the amazing people at NSF/ASC who played their part, big and small, in helping make this a life-changing experience: my handler on the Ice, Elaine Hood; my coordinator, Samina Ouda; the Hawaiians (my AAW teammates), Kirsten Carlson and Michelle Schwengel-Regala; my roommate, Scott Landsdolt; the AAWP director, Valentine Kass; diver and friend Henry Kaiser; co-explorer Jerod Knox; documentarian Mike Lucibella; my hosts at the McMurdo dive locker, Rob Robbins and Steve Rupp; my hosts at Lake Hoare, Nurse Beth and Tirzah; my hosts at Cape Royds (lead penguins Katie and Jean); Arrival Heights Neil and the folks at Crary Labs; all the hundreds of amazing support personnel at McMurdo; microbiologist Sam Bowser; and artist Laura Von Rosk. And thank you to the people I bonded with or interviewed along the way: the legendary Rae Spain; Brian Atkinson, the paleobotanist; Kim Roush, the grad student; Moo man Paul A. Cziko; LTER Peter Doran; Nick Santos; Jennifer Bault; Todd Zatorski; Ken Sims (aka Magma Man); Kirsty Tinto and the Rosetta team; Jay Rotella and the seal team; Britney Schmidt and Ice Fin; Brian "Supertiger" Rauch; David Meyer, the long duration balloon fabricator; Kory and Steve, the traverse team leaders; Zoe, the engineer/mountaineer; Drew, the Kiwi diver; Dr. Chris at General Hospital; Dustin the fireman; Amelia the health clinician/janitor; Tony at vehicles; and BBC cinematographers Espen, Hugh, and John. Finally, thanks to Aunt Karen Shaffer and all the artists and writers at AAWC. Big shout-out to the thousands of students who saw and reacted to my Antarctica presentations, which led me to scrap my ginormous graphic novel in favor of this much shorter and potent book of wonder.

And thanks to everyone at Candlewick: my wonderful longtime editor Andrea Tompa, designer Carolynn DeCillo, Juan Botero, copyeditor Jason Emmanuel, and proofreader Emily Quill. Thanks to my main man and agent, Edward Necarsulmer IV (who seemed in awe when I showed him this idea), and, of course, my favorite comic book illustrator, Corban Wilkin!

Most of all, thank you to my dad, who didn't live long enough to see this but loved hearing about it, to my mom, and to my family, Maggie and Zola, who were halfway around the world in their own frozen land called Montreal.

DEDICATED TO THE MEMORY OF MARK MacMILLAN

PHOTO CREDITS

INDEX